KU-340-859

BRITAIN SINCE 1930

Life at Work

Philip Sauvain

Fordson Tractors

WAYLAND

BRITAIN SINCE 1930

The Advance of Technology
Leisure Time
Life at Home
Life at Work

DONCASTER LIBRARY AND INFORMATION SERVICE	
014956243	
J M L S	15/12/96
J942.083	£8.99

Cover pictures: *Above* An assembly line in a Morris car factory in 1945. *Below left* A modern car factory with no workers in sight – only robots! *Below right* A woman police officer in the 1990s.

Title page: An advert for Fordson tractors in 1937. Using a tractor, a farmer could plough in an hour, the same amount that would take all day using horses.

Contents page: A farmer ploughing with horses in the 1930s.

Series editor: Francesca Motisi
Series designer: Joyce Chester

First published in 1995 by
Wayland (Publishers) Ltd
61, Western Road, Hove
East Sussex BN3 1JD, England

© Copyright 1995 Wayland (Publishers) Limited

British Library Cataloguing in Publication Data
Sauvain, Philip
  Life at work . - (Britain since 1930 Series)
  I. Title II. Series
  331.0941

ISBN 0-7502-1638-7

Printed and bound by B.P.C. Paulton Books, Great Britain

Picture acknowledgements
The publishers would like to thank the following for allowing their pictures to be reproduced in this book: Hulton Deutsch *cover* (above), 6 (above), 8 (below), 17 (above), 19 (below), 20, 21 (above), 22 (centre), 26; Imperial War Museum 24 *Ruby Loftus screwing a breech ring* by Dame Laura Knight, 25 Second World War Poster – Agriculture and Food; Manchester City Art Gallery 5 *An Organ Grinder* – Holgate St., Hulme, Manchester, by Laurence Stephen Lowry, 1934, oil on canvas; Francesca Motisi 15 (below); National Railway Museum/Science and Society 8 Poster of *The Permanent Way* by Stanhope Forbes, 1924; Popperfoto 4 (below); copyright is held by the Rural History Centre, University of Reading *title and contents pages;* Sainsbury's 19 (above); Philip Sauvain 4 (above), 6 (below), 7 (both), 11 (both), 14 (both), 15 (above), 16, 17 (below), 21 (below), 23, 28 (centre); Spectrum Colour Library 29 (right); Tony Stone Worldwide *cover* (below left), 9 (above/Drew Jimson), 27; Topham Picturepoint 10 (above), 25, 13 (both), 18, 22 (above and below), 28 (left); Wayland Picture Library *cover* (bottom right).

Contents

Out of work

Old children's toys and games sometimes tell us about the past. These Snap playing cards show the work people did fifty to sixty years ago. A policeman controls traffic with his arms. A coalman delivers coal. To be realistic, however, the game might have had an extra worker with the title 'OUT OF WORK'. This was the time known as the Great Depression when over two million workers in South Wales, around Glasgow and in the north of England were unemployed.

⇧ An old card game, Snap, with pictures of workers in the 1930s.

⇦ Unemployed cotton workers queuing outside the Labour Exchange in Oldham.

Diary of an unemployed man in 1935	
Breakfast:	Bread and margarine. Tea.
Morning:	Queues up on Thursdays at the Labour Exchange to collect his dole of 25s [£1.25]. His wife takes the money to pay for rent, gas and food. By Monday most of it has gone.
Midday:	Meal of bread, soup and potatoes. His wife sometimes buys a pig's head and boils it, removing the bones. It keeps the family in meat for a week.
Afternoon:	Goes to the reading room in the library to look for a job in the newspapers. No luck. Wanders aimlessly through the streets.
Supper:	Bread and margarine. Tea.

Two out of every three workers were unemployed in the Rhondda in South Wales. The writer J. B. Priestley saw towns like this along the River Tyne in 1933.

Jarrow

'One out of every two shops appeared to be permanently closed. Wherever we went there were men hanging about, not scores of them but hundreds and thousands of them.'

Hebburn

'Here again, idle men hung about the streets. Nothing, it seemed, would ever happen here again.'

Many of the cotton workers in ⇨ Salford, Lancashire, were out of work during the Great Depression. This painting by Lowry shows a street scene in 1934.

Your older relatives may have stories to tell about the Great Depression, like this one recalled by a woman in the Potteries (Stoke-on-Trent).

> *'Men were funny in those days. Very proud. They thought it was their job to be the breadwinner. Father used to tell us about a distant relative whose dole [unemployment benefit] had been cut to 8 shillings [40p] a week because his daughters were both working and living at home. So when Christmas came, they bought the chicken, jellies and ham. On Christmas Day he wouldn't eat a thing. He was so ashamed his daughters had provided the treat and not himself.'*

⇧ An election poster in 1931 showing the effects of unemployment on people in Britain.

There were well-paid jobs in the 1930s, but these were mainly in the South-east and Midlands. Sales of cars, radios and household goods were booming there. Many new factories were built before the Second World War, like those in the photograph opposite. They used electricity instead of coal, so could be built anywhere in Britain. Most were built close to a main road and near a large town.

⇦ An advert for a Ford motor car in 1938. Fords were made at a huge motor works in Dagenham near London.

Unemployment ended with the outbreak of war in 1939. After 1945, too, there was plenty of work available. This is why many people from India, Pakistan and the Caribbean came to Britain in the 1950s in search of a job.

⇧ Factories along London's North Circular Road in 1958.

Labour Exchanges tried to help workers get jobs. We call them job centres today. ⇩

By the 1970s, however, life in Britain was changing fast. More and more people wanted central heating instead of a coal fire in their homes. Plastics were being used more instead of steel. Cloth made from synthetic fibres, such as viscose and polyester, competed with wool and cotton. Foreign cars, radios and television sets took trade away from British firms. Some factories closed down or employed fewer workers. Computers did jobs which many people had done in the past. As a result by the 1980s, over two million workers were unemployed once again.

Working conditions

Working conditions on the railways, in factories and in coal mines were very different in the 1930s compared with today. People expected to work long hours for low wages. One millworker said her day began at 7 am and ended at 5.15 pm. She worked four hours on Saturdays and had a week's holiday a year. Working in a factory, mill or colliery took a lot out of the workers employed there.

⇧ A railway company poster in 1924 showing maintenance workers. Notice the number of workers in the picture. Many more people were employed to do a job in the 1920s and 1930s compared with today. There were fewer labour-saving devices then.

A Lancashire cotton mill

'The noise from a thousand looms is indescribable and very frightening for a beginner. Conversation is impossible except by lip-reading.'

⇐ A modern textile mill. Conditions are much quieter nowadays.

A coal mine in the 1930s

'Almost all the men in the village were miners and were easily recognizable by their pale faces and blue scars on hands and faces. The older miners walked with a stoop and with shortness of breath – a sure sign of silicosis.'

First day in a coal mine

'I reported to the lamp room and joined the others on the 'spake', the train of trolleys which took us down the main drift of the colliery. We sat three to a seat holding our heads tightly on our knees. It grew blacker and blacker. I was petrified. Then we walked – it seemed miles – to the coal face. That first day did eventually come to an end. We placed our shirts back on our sweaty bodies caked with dust and trudged wearily towards the drift and back to the surface. Oh! how lovely it was to breathe fresh air, to see the sun and hear the birds, to be able to stand up straight.'

Miners coming off their shift in the early 1940s. ⇨

There were many industrial accidents in the past. Mining disasters were much more common then than they are now. Eighty miners died in a Derbyshire pit disaster in 1950 and another eighty-three died at Easington in County Durham the following year.

⇧ A miner at the coal face in about 1940. Instead of using a coal-cutting machine, he uses a pick. Notice the absence of protective clothing – he does not even have a hard hat to protect his head.

> # 261 MINERS PERISH IN BLAZING PIT
>
> ## OFFICIAL STATEMENT LAST NIGHT: "NO PERSON CAN BE ALIVE"
>
> ### RESCUERS WITHDRAWN AND SHAFT SEALED UP
>
> 3 Men Give Lives For Comrades
>
> Boots Burned Off On Red-Hot Roads

⇦ Headlines in *The Daily Telegraph* for 24 September 1934 after the Gresford Colliery disaster in North Wales.

Working conditions have much improved since the 1930s. Pithead baths enabled miners to leave work looking smart instead of caked in coal dust. By 1980, most people worked a much shorter working week. Few worked on Saturday mornings. Instead of leaving school at fourteen, young people had to stay at school until they were sixteen.

In 1984 an ex-miner summed up the changes in his industry in 1984 compared to 1917

'Coal-mining today is vastly different to what it was when I started in the pits back in 1917. Today men are working under a steel canopy. The picks and hatchets are gone. It's the machines that cut and load the coal. It is more like a factory.'

⇧ Dodworth Colliery in Barnsley in 1971. The pit has since been closed and all traces removed – apart from the slag heap in the distance.

⇧ Modern factories often have excellent facilities for their workers, such as a canteen, clinic and nursery. This photograph, taken in 1960, shows the sports ground used by workers in a fertilizer factory in Norfolk.

Working on a farm

↑ Harvesting corn in the 1930s, using a reaper binder in Cornwall.

The Great Depression in the 1930s affected farmworkers as well. Some were sacked because farmers got so little for their crops, they couldn't afford to keep them on. Many of those who remained worked fifty hours for less than £2 a week. Farmworkers' cottages had few modern conveniences then. As late as the 1960s, many were still lit by paraffin lamps and had only an earth toilet inside. You took a bath in front of the fire – in a tin tub filled with hot water from a kettle!

During the Second World War, many farm jobs were done by women in the Land Army (see the poster on page 25). By this time, farmers were buying tractors and machines to save labour. There were well over one million farmworkers in 1946. Today there are fewer than 300,000.

New types of seeds, fertilizers and pesticides, together with more efficient methods using tractors and labour-saving machines, helped farmers produce much more corn, meat and milk than they did in 1930. Some of these changes are highlighted in the accounts which follow. They were written by a woman who grew up as a child on a small farm in Yorkshire in the 1940s and 1950s.

Ploughing

'Dad used to plough with two horses, Dolly and Prince. The land was quite steep, so he could only plough a single furrow at a time. He walked behind holding the reins and also holding the two wooden handles of the plough to steer it in a straight line. It took quite a lot of strength to do this as well as a lot of skill. Ploughing also took a lot out of the horses. They could only plough so much in a day.'

⇧ Threshing in the 1930s at Gatton, Surrey.

⇦ Ploughing fields in 1936, Kingsdown, Kent.

13

Dairying

'Until 1958, when we got electricity, Dad and the farmer-man [farmworker] milked the cows by hand into small pails, sitting on three-legged stools. It took them at least an hour to milk sixteen cows. At night and on winter mornings they lit paraffin lamps to light up the cowshed. The milk was later poured through strainers into milk churns which a dairy lorry collected the next day.'

⇧ Hand-milking in the late 1950s on a farm with only one or two cows.

⇐ Milk churns on a donkey cart in Ireland in 1965.

Haymaking

'We cut the grass with a mowing machine pulled by horses. You had to gather the loose hay and make it into haycocks before it was loaded on to the hay carts. It was horrible work. The hay was prickly, the dust stuck in your throat, and there were hordes of insects around the horses.'

Harvesting

'At harvest-time we cut the corn with a machine which bound it into sheaves. We stood six of them on end against each other to make stooks and left them in the field to dry in the sun. They were later carted away and piled high in cornstacks at the side of the farmyard. On threshing days throughout the winter, all the neighbouring farmers and farmworkers came to help. Until 1946, we hired a steam traction engine and threshing machine to do the job. It took twelve people to do the work – tending the machine, lifting bales of straw and bags of corn, and fetching coal and buckets of water [to make the steam]. After the Second World War, we got a diesel-powered tractor to do the same job. Then, one day in the early 1970s, one man driving a combine harvester and another on a tractor alongside – pulling a wagon to collect the corn – did the work it had taken twelve men a week to do only thirty years earlier! Few farmers needed farmworkers then!'

⇧ A steam traction engine at Beamish Museum, County Durham. There may be an engine like this at a museum near you.

A combine harvester in the 1990s. Compare this with the harvest scenes on pages 12 and 13. ⇩

Working in a shop

We know what it was like to work in a shop in the 1930s from photographs and also from adverts, posters and documents, such as the stock list (below) kept by the manager of a furnishing store in 1928.

⇐ This stock list was drawn up each year to calculate the value of the stock left in the shop. The prices tell us about the cost of furnishing a home at that time. If you compared them with prices today, you could work out how much they have risen in the last sixty years or so.

Stock Jan 31	1928		
1 Bedroom suite	15	10	.
1 - -	12	10	
1 Chesterfield	18		.
1 Sideboard	6		
3	9	15	.
2 Wicker Chairs	1	14	6
1 Dining Table	3	12	6
2 Tables	3	.	.
6 Pedestals	2	17	6
13 Cornise Poles	1	12	.
1 Bookcase	3	5	.
4 Bedsteads	15	15	.
6 Flock Mattresses	5	17	.
2 Fibre "	1	10	.
1 Straw .		10	
2 Feather Beds	5	14	0
4 Spring Mattress	4	10	.
6 Chairs	1	10	
5	3	.	.

⇐ Serving a customer by aid of candlelight during a power cut in 1937.

Advertising plates like this one were screwed to the wall of a grocer's shop. ⇓

In 1930, the assistants in a grocer's shop had to weigh and measure everything they sold. Few products were ready packaged as they are today. This is why shopping for groceries took much longer than it does today. A Suffolk woman recalled those days.

> 'The grocery and hardware shop sold everything from butter to boot polish, custard powder and coal shovels. Almost all the commodities were sold loose – sugar, tea, dried fruit, biscuits etc were weighed and bagged for each customer, while butter was cut from a large block, as was cooking salt. Goods were paid for at a cash desk in the centre of the shop.'

Many shops delivered the goods you bought. Street traders in one Suffolk village in the 1930s included *'a muffin man, a winkle seller and a man who came round with rabbits strung on sticks.'* Paraffin for cooking and lighting was also delivered, as well as milk, vegetables and bread.

Working in a baker's shop

'My day started at 5 am, weighing up dough until 7 am. Then I had to go delivering hot rolls to the gentry's houses. I was a small boy and could not see over the large basket on the front of the bike. Back to the bakehouse, a quick roll and butter, a cup of drink, then school by 9 am, invariably late. I did deliveries again in school dinner-time then, after school, I worked in the bakehouse, with a break for tea, until it was time for bed.'

⇧ Milk was delivered by horse and cart in 1930. The milkman filled your can or jug from his churn.

When manufacturers began to put their tea, sugar and butter in packets in the 1930s, fewer shop assistants were needed. Small shops had already begun to face competition from the big chain stores. Woolworth and Marks and Spencer were opening twenty-five to fifty new shops a year in the 1930s.

Shop assistants in the big stores were proud of their work and took great care with their appearance. A shop assistant in Rochdale in Lancashire recalled his days working in the Co-op in the 1930s.

'Compared with working in a textile mill, you were like royalty. Everybody in the Street knew that you were working at Co-op and that you'd got in with it and you were treated like royalty. Everybody said he's working at Co-op.'

⇐ Sainsbury's grocery store in 1931.

A fashionable department store in Harrogate in 1938. ⇓

Lionel Harrisson, who had worked as an assistant in a big London department store, was interviewed on television in 1984.

'Oh we had to look like proper little gentlemen. We had black jackets, striped trousers, spats, black shoes, stiff white collar, and a sober-coloured tie. And the shop walkers were always in morning dress. The head shop walker was a god. We were all scared stiff of him.'

The Second World War had a big effect on shops and shoppers. Food and clothes were rationed to make sure that everyone got a fair share. Shop assistants had to check coupons in the ration book, as well as taking money for the goods they sold. They also had to put up with the complaints of many customers who queued for hours outside the shop.

From the war diary of a Warwickshire woman

'Friday 18 July 1941. In Leamington this morning we had a good deal to do and shopping takes a long time. People take their ration books to the shops and they have to have the coupons cancelled as well as being served with bits of this and that.'

⇧ Queuing for food at the start of the Second World War.

Worse still, rationing continued for nine years after the end of the war. When it finally ended in 1954, the way was clear at last for the new supermarkets which were beginning to open in Britain. People served themselves and paid for their purchases when they left the shop. Prices were often much cheaper in the supermarkets. People stopped going to the village shop or to the corner shop near their homes. Supermarket chains, such as Tesco, Sainsbury's, Waitrose and Asda, took the place of many small groceries, butchers, bakers and greengrocers.

As a result, the work of the shop assistant changed. Instead of serving customers one by one, shopworkers spent much of their time stacking shelves or sitting at a till at the exit. Being a shop assistant was no longer the interesting job, meeting and talking to customers, that it had been fifty years earlier.

Retired shop assistant in 1984

'When self-service got really going, I didn't have the same job satisfaction I had as a shop assistant.'

In the last ten or twenty years or so, there have been many other new developments. Many town centres have been blocked off to become shopping precincts like the one in the picture. In some areas, huge shopping centres under the same roof have been built on sites on the outskirts of a city. Shopping malls like this include the Metro Centre in Tyneside, Meadowhall in Sheffield and Brent Cross in north London.

⇧ Britain's first supermarket was opened in 1948.

A shopping precinct in King's Lynn, Norfolk, in 1975. ⇩

Women at work

Until 1900, women were expected to take second place to men. Few women held jobs of any importance. Those who had jobs gave them up when they got married. By 1930, however, this was changing. Many more women were working in offices, shops and department stores, or in the new factories making luxury goods.

⇧ A policewoman in uniform in 1930.

⇧ Women workers in a canning factory in 1929.

A craftswoman at work in 1932 making tennis rackets. ⇨

Daily timetable of a housemaid

06.30: Rise. Clean grates and lay fires, sweep carpets and dust in dining room, library, billiard room, drawing room, morning room. Sweep and dust and polish floors and staircases.

08.00: Breakfast in servants' hall.

09.00: Start bedrooms. Help with bed-making, empty dirty water, refill jugs. Clean grates and lay fires. Fill up coal boxes and wood baskets. Sweep and dust. Clean bathrooms. Change into afternoon uniform.

13.00: Lunch in servants' hall.

14.00: Clean silver, brass, water cans, trim lamps.

16.00: Tea in servants' hall.

17.00: Light fires in bedrooms.

18.00: Cans of hot water to bedrooms.

19.30: Turn down beds, make up fires and empty dirty water. Fill up coal and wood containers. Leave morning trays set in housemaid's pantry.

Until 1939, however, the usual job for a working woman without qualifications was that of a servant. Girls left school at fourteen and went into service. This was very hard work.

A page from the Army and Navy store's catalogue for 1933. It is advertising caps and aprons for servants. ⇨

SERVANTS' CAPS AND APRONS.

A.D.G. 501
White Lawn Apron, in a very good quality, trimmed scalloped edging .. 2/6
Coronet Cap to match, trimmed black velvet.. .. .. .. 1/6
Collar and Cuffs to match 1/11½

A.D.G. 506
Plain Apron, with round or square bibs, and large pockets 2/11, 3/6, 4/11
Sister Dora Cap, plain
In White Muslin 1/1
In White Linen 2/1

A.D.G. 503
Plain White Muslin Apron, with wide double hem .. 2/11
Coronet Cap to match, finished black velvet .. 1/8
Collar and Cuffs to match, the set 1/6

A.D.G. 504
White Check Muslin Tea Apron, trimmed lace .. 1/11½
Cap to match, finished black velvet 1/6
Collar and Cuffs to match, the set 1/7

A.D.G. 502
Beige or White Organdi Apron, trimmed lace 4/6
Coronet Cap to match, trimmed black velvet 1/11½
Collar and Cuffs to match, the set 2/6

A.D.G. 505
Afternoon Apron, trimmed embroidery 2/11
Sister Dora Cap, with elastic at back, trimmed veining 1/5

A.D.G. 500
Afternoon Apron, of good quality Lawn, trimmed embroidery 4/3
Cap with Embroidered Front, trimmed black velvet 1/11½

A.D.G. 507
White Spotted Muslin Apron, with plain hem .. 2/11
Cap to match, with elastic at back for short hair 2/6
Collar and Cuffs to match 1/11

ALL PRICES ARE SUBJECT TO MARKET FLUCTUATIONS.

After 1945, however, many former servants were no longer prepared to do the work. Winnie Whitehouse, who had served in the armed forces, explained why in a television programme in 1990.

'We felt we were as good as they were. We didn't mind the work. It was just having to kow-tow to people that'd been sat at home all the while.'

A number of things made it easier for women to go out to work. Families were much smaller. Many more homes had mains electricity. More people were able to buy labour-saving domestic appliances, such as a washing machine and a vacuum cleaner. Women found they could keep the house clean, cook the meals and still have time to go out to work. Many more men were prepared to share the housework and look after the children. During the Second World War, women workers were recruited in their millions to work in factories making radar, tanks, uniforms and other wartime goods.

⇧ This picture of Ruby Loftus, a highly skilled engineering worker, was painted in 1943. It was later used on wartime posters to encourage other women to volunteer for similar work in factories.

Women volunteers were also recruited as Land Army girls to grow more food for Britain. They had to put up with a hard, back-breaking job, often living in a primitive cottage without electricity, running water or a bathroom.

By 1951 roughly 25% of married women were employed. Ten years later, the proportion had risen to 33%. In 1985 women formed over 40% of the country's workforce. Laws had been passed giving them the right to equal pay and preventing employers from promoting men instead of similarly qualified women. What is more, they were allowed time off from their jobs to have a baby, unlike the women of an earlier generation.

Wartime recruitment poster. ⇩

'I worked for two years after getting married but gave my job up (as a secretary) to have a baby. That was in 1960. Fifteen years later, after both my children had started at the comprehensive, I trained as a teacher. Attitudes to married women working had changed a lot in that time. I soon noticed the difference. Equal pay for women had come in and many of my colleagues at school were women in their forties like me. Lucky I did get a job, too. We'd never have bought this house on one income alone.'

Automation

By 1930, new methods were being used in British factories to make cars and radios. All the things needed to make the product were put together by a team of workers on either side of a moving belt or platform called a production line. It was a more efficient form of manufacture but the work was often boring and monotonous for the workers on the line.

A motor car assembly line in 1945. ⇩

A motor car factory in 1933

'I was taken through various huge sheds in which hundreds and hundreds of mechanics were at work making and testing parts. All these sheds were the same with fly-wheels above and brown-overalled men below. Every man was limited to one job but there was a certain amount of variety inside the job. This was not strictly mass production: there was no endless moving chain; there were no men restricted to putting on a bolt there, a nut here.'

Making something work automatically is called automation. When machines that did this were introduced into mines, factories and farms, they made it possible for employers to cut down on the number of workers they had to take on. Many people lost their jobs as Arthur Amis, a Norfolk farmworker, recalled on BBC Television in 1984.

'Well, I really didn't mind the machinery as far as that goes but I felt it when men had to leave. I didn't like men having to leave a job because automation was coming. This was inevitable but we had to accept it.'

Some jobs could now be done automatically by robots, such as in the car industry. We think of this as a modern development, but as long ago as 1933, *Punch* magazine printed a cartoon showing a robot saying to his employer: *'Master, I can do the work of fifty men.'* His employer replies: *'Yes I know that. But who is to support the fifty men?'* Since then, robots have been programmed by computers to carry out many tasks, such as spot welding, with great precision and accuracy. Robots have a number of advantages. They can work continuously for twenty-four hours a day. They do not need tea or lunch breaks. They do not go on strike and they can be easily scrapped when they are no longer needed.

⇧ Car bodies moving down a modern welding production line operated by robots.

Robots do have some disadvantages. Like all machines, they can develop faults. Unlike human workers, they are not easily replaced if they break down and they cannot use common sense to solve a problem. Arthur Barker, a maintenance worker, explained the effect of automation on the workers in the chemical industry in 1984.

'The process worker had to become a bloke that knew instruments and how to use instruments because the machinery was geared that way. Machines were getting programmed and things like that. Whereas years ago it only needed someone with a bit of muscle.'

⇐ Smoke from pottery kilns belching into the sky at Stoke-on-Trent in 1910.

When this photograph of Stoke-on-Trent was taken in 1960, the coal-burning beehive kilns used to fire pottery were being replaced and the collieries were closing. You can tell this from the absence of smoke compared with the photograph above taken fifty years earlier. ⇨

A number of the old beehive pottery kilns have been preserved, such as here at the Gladstone Pottery Museum in Stoke-on-Trent. Notice the clear blue sky. ⇨

The use of automation has meant that many processes are controlled today by electric switches and computers. Electric power turns machines. Electric furnaces melt metals. Electric kilns bake pottery. Sixty years ago, electricity was only just beginning to take the place of coal as a source of power. As you saw in Chapter One, the change-over from coal to electricity resulted in the loss of many jobs in the mines. But it had one great advantage. It made the industrial towns much cleaner – as you can see from these photographs of the potteries.

Glossary

Automation Machinery that works on its own without needing the constant attention of a worker.

Chain store One of a group of shops selling the same products and owned by the same company.

Combine harvester Farm machine that automatically cuts and threshes corn and binds the straw as it moves across a cornfield.

Dole (Unemployment Benefit) Money paid by the government to people out of work.

Domestic appliance A tool or machine used to do work in the house, such as a vacuum cleaner, refrigerator or food processor.

Drift A tunnel in a coal mine, often running from the surface to deep underground.

Equal pay This is when men and women are paid the same for doing the same work.

Great Depression The period of the 1930s when there was a high level of unemployment in Britain.

In service Being employed as a servant.

Job centre Local office that stores details of vacant jobs and aims to help people find employment.

Job satisfaction Taking pride in doing your work.

Labour Exchange Old name for a Job Centre.

Labour-saving device A machine which reduces the amount of human effort needed to do a job, such as a combine harvester on a farm or a dishwasher in the kitchen.

Land Army Organization that recruited women to work on farms during the Second World War.

Mass production Method of using machines and labour to make large quantities of a product.

Production line System where all the jobs needed to make something are done in turn by a team of workers as the product passes along a moving belt or platform.

Protective clothing These are special clothes, such as hard hats, goggles and heavy boots, worn by workers to protect themselves from injury.

Ration book In the Second World War this was a book containing coupons which entitled the owner to a fixed amount of food, petrol or clothing.

Robot A machine that can perform tasks automatically without help from an operator.

Shopping mall A vast complex of different shops and restaurants all housed inside the same building.

Shopping precinct Streets of shops that can only be visited by people on foot. Vehicles delivering goods are only allowed to enter the area when the shops are closed to customers.

Silicosis A disease caused by breathing in particles of grit, such as coal dust.

Synthetic fibres The raw material for different types of cloth made from chemicals which have been taken from substances such as coal, oil and wood.

Threshing Beating stalks of wheat, barley and other types of corn to separate the ears (containing flour) from the husks and straw.

Books to read

Behind the Main Street by Kenneth Hudson (Bodley Head, 1982)
How We Used To Live, 1954-1970 by Freda Kelsall (A & C Black, 1987)
Looking Back: Work by Philip Sauvain (Wayland 1991)
We Were There: 1930s by Rosemary Rees (Heinemann, 1993)
We Were There: 1940s by Rosemary Rees (Heinemann, 1993)
We Were There: 1950s by Rosemary Rees (Heinemann, 1993)
We Were There: 1960s by Rosemary Rees (Heinemann, 1993)
We Were There: 1970s by Rosemary Rees (Heinemann, 1993)
We Were There: 1980s by Rosemary Rees (Heinemann, 1993)
Working Lives: Shops by Cherry Gilchrist (Batsford, 1987)
Working Lives: The Coal Mines by Nathaniel Harris (Batsford, 1987)
Working Lives: The Railway Industry by Betty Williams (Batsford, 1987)
Working Lives: The Textile Industry by Judy Slinn (Batsford, 1987)

Acknowledgements

Grateful acknowledgement is given for permission to reprint copyright material:

Page 5 From *English Journey,* by J. B. Priestley, Heinemann, 1934

Page 8 From an essay by Marjorie Tattersall in *In Those Days*, edited by Julia Thorogood, copyright Age Concern Essex, Sarsen Publishing, 1994

Page 9 (both quotes) From an essay by Glyn Jeffreys in *In Those Days*, edited by Julia Thorogood, copyright Age Concern Essex, Sarsen Publishing, 1994

Page 11 From BBC Television programme *All Our Working Lives:Coal in 1984*

Page 17 From *Suffolk: Within Living Memory*, compiled by the Suffolk Federation of Women's Institutes, Countryside Books and the Suffolk East and Suffolk West Federations of Women's Institutes, 1994

Page 18 (above) From an essay by George Cook in *In Those Days*, edited by Julia Thorogood, copyright Age Concern Essex, Sarsen Publishing, 1994

Page 18 (below) and Page 19 From BBC Television series *All Our Working Lives*, 1984

Page 20 From *Mrs Milburn's Diaries*, edited by Peter Donnelly, Harrap, 1979

Page 21 From BBC Television series *All Our Working Lives*, 1984

Page 24 From BBC Television series *Now The War Is Over*, 1990

Page 27 (above) From *English Journey* by J.B. Priestley, Heinemann, 1934

Page 27 (below) From BBC Television series *All Our Working Lives,* 1984

Page 28 From BBC Television programme *All Our Working Lives: Chemicals*, 1984.

While every effort has been made to trace copyright holders, the publishers apologise for any inadvertent omissions.

Index